Exceptional African Americans

Harriet TUBMAN

Hero of the Underground Railroad

Charlotte Taylor
and
Stephen Feinstein

Enslow Publishing
101 W. 23rd Street
Suite 240
New York, NY 10011
USA
enslow.com

Words to Know

abolitionist—A person who was against slavery.

Civil War—The war fought between the Northern and Southern states of America from 1861 to 1865.

conductor—On the Underground Railroad, a person who helped slaves escape.

crops—Plants that are grown by farmers for food or other uses.

North Star—A bright star that can be seen in the sky when a person looks to the north.

overseer—A person who was in charge of the slaves working in the fields.

plantation—A large farm in the South.

slave—A person who works for someone else against his or her will.

station—A house along the Underground Railroad where an escaping slave could stay safe.

Underground Railroad—A system set up to help slaves move to freedom in the North.

Union—The name for the North during the Civil War.

Contents

Harriet Tubman

CHAPTER 1

Life as a Slave

Harriet Tubman was born a **slave** around 1820. Her parents named her Araminta, but everyone called her Minty. Minty's parents, Harriet and Benjamin Ross, were slaves also. They lived with their eleven children on a **plantation** in Maryland. The family belonged to the owner of the plantation.

Life was hard for the slaves on the plantation. They worked in the fields from morning until night. They never had enough to eat and they were always tired. Slaves were not paid for their work.

The **overseer** beat them with a whip if they did not do their work fast enough.

Minty Runs Away

When Minty was about six, she was sent out to work at other plantations. She had many jobs, like cleaning, sewing, and taking care of babies.

Harriet Says:

"I prayed to God to make me strong and able to fight,...and that's what I've always prayed for ever since."

It was hard work, and she missed her family very much. One time, Minty ran away. She hid for a few days in a pigpen. When she returned to the house, she was sick. She could not do much work. Minty was soon sent back to her family on the old plantation.

Slaves were whipped if they did not do as they were told.

CHAPTER 2

Harriet Makes Up Her Mind

Once she was feeling better, Minty was sent to work in the fields. She spent her days picking **crops** like cotton and corn. Even though the work was hard, she enjoyed being outside. As the years went by, Minty became as strong as many of the men.

One day, Minty saw a slave running away. The slave's overseer told Minty to stop him, but she did not. The overseer picked up a heavy weight and threw it at the slave. It missed him, but it hit

Plantations were very large farms. Slaves worked in the houses and out in the fields.

Slaves were bought and sold at auctions like these.

Minty in the head. She was very badly hurt. Minty survived, but her head bothered her for the rest of her life.

Minty hated being a slave. Two of her sisters were sold to another plantation. She was afraid that one day she would be sold and would never see her family again.

TO BE SOLD on board the Ship *Bance-Iſland*, on tueſday the 6th of *May* next, at *Aſhley-Ferry*; a choice cargo of about 250 fine healthy

NEGROES,

juſt arrived from the Windward & Rice Coaſt. —The utmoſt care has already been taken, and ſhall be continued, to keep them free from the leaſt danger of being infected with the SMALL-POX, no boat having been on board, and all other communication with people from *Charles-Town* prevented.

Auſtin, Laurens, & Appleby.

N. B. Full one Half of the above Negroes have had the SMALL-POX in their own Country.

This notice describes a group of slaves who will be sold at an auction.

A Married Woman

In 1844, Minty married John Tubman, a free black man. Around this time, she changed her name. She was now Harriet Tubman. Harriet wanted to be free. She began to dream of escaping to the North. In the North, black people lived in freedom. But her husband did not share her dreams. So Harriet made up her mind. She knew it would be dangerous, but she had to try. She would run away to the North.

Harriet Says:

"Every great dream begins with a dreamer."

CHAPTER 3

Escape!

Harriet's owner died in 1849. She was afraid that now she would be sold to a plantation far away. The time had come for her to make a break for freedom.

Two of Harriet's brothers decided to go with her. They took off together, but soon her brothers became scared. It was dark, and they did not know where they were going. The three of them returned home, but Harriet did not give up on her dream. She would make the trip on her own.

The Underground Railroad

Harriet knew that some white people who were against slavery helped runaway slaves escape. These people were called **abolitionists**. The secret way to the North was called the **Underground Railroad**. Friendly homes were called **stations**.

The people who worked on the Underground Railroad thought slaves should be free.

One night, Harriet slipped away from the plantation. She did not have a map so she used the **North Star** as a guide. Harriet walked all night through the woods. She stopped at her first station in Bucktown, Maryland.

Every night she walked many miles through woods and swamp. During the day, she hid in Underground Railroad stations. Harriet finally reached Pennsylvania, a free state. She had made it!

Harriet Says:

"I looked at my hands to see if I was the same person...I felt like I was in heaven."

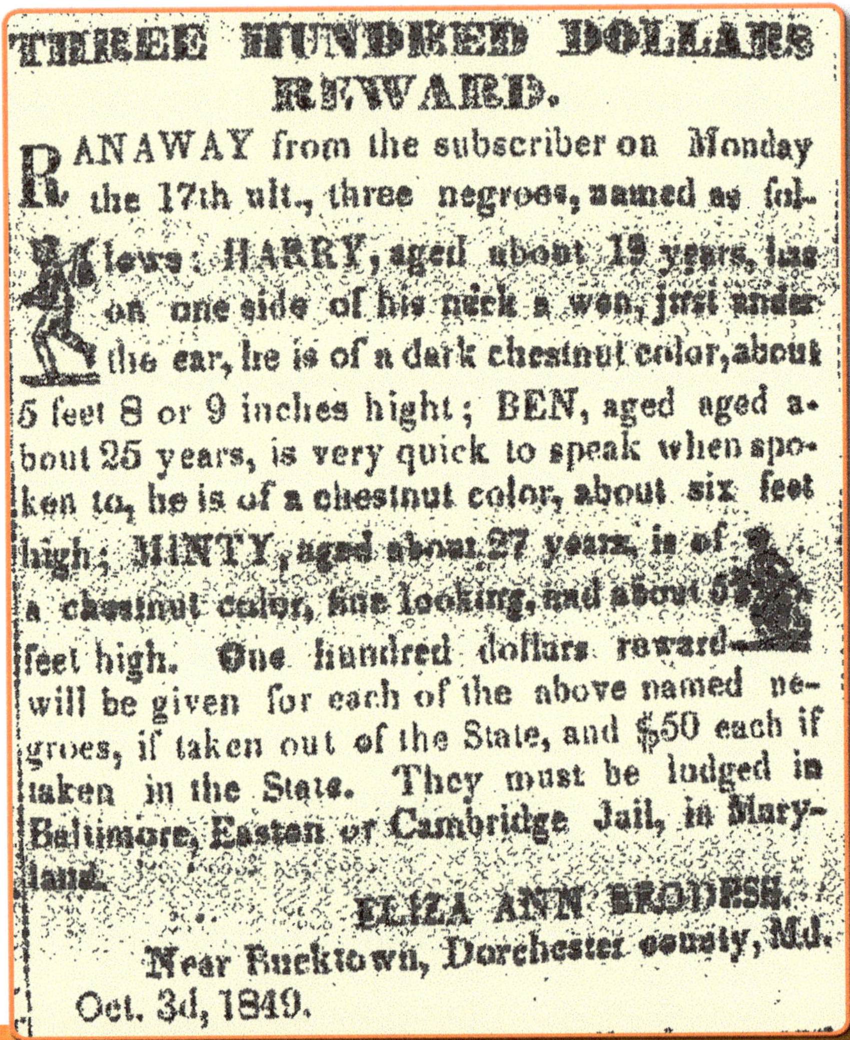

THREE HUNDRED DOLLARS REWARD.

RANAWAY from the subscriber on Monday the 17th ult., three negroes, named as follows: HARRY, aged about 19 years, has on one side of his neck a wen, just under the ear, he is of a dark chestnut color, about 5 feet 8 or 9 inches hight; BEN, aged aged about 25 years, is very quick to speak when spoken to, he is of a chestnut color, about six feet high; MINTY, aged about 27 years, is of a chestnut color, fine looking, and about 5 feet high. One hundred dollars reward will be given for each of the above named negroes, if taken out of the State, and $50 each if taken in the State. They must be lodged in Baltimore, Easton or Cambridge Jail, in Maryland.

ELIZA ANN BRODESS.
Near Bucktown, Dorchester county, Md.
Oct. 3d, 1849.

Harriet's owner offered a reward for her capture in 1849. The reward was one hundred dollars.

CHAPTER 4

A Free Woman

Now that she was free, Harriet needed to make money. She worked as a cook and house cleaner. But Harriet never forgot the people she had left behind. Over the next few years, she made many trips back to Maryland. She became a **conductor** on the Underground Railroad.

Harriet faced great danger. There was a big reward offered for her capture. Harriet knew that she would be killed or put in jail if she were caught. But this did not stop her.

Harriet led the slaves across mountains, rivers, and forests. Many people helped along the way

Abolitionist Harriet Tubman provided safe houses for escaping slaves. Harriet is standing at the far left.

with food and shelter. Harriet probably led several hundred slaves, including her family, to freedom in the North.

War Breaks Out

The **Civil War** began in 1861. Northern states wanted to end slavery. Southern states wanted to keep slaves. The two sides fought for years and many people died. During the war, Harriet was a nurse and a spy for the **Union** army. President Abraham Lincoln finally decided to free the slaves.

Harriet Tubman spoke to crowds about her work on the Underground Railroad.

The Emancipation Proclamation said that slaves should be freed.

The war ended in 1865. By then, Harriet had bought land in Auburn, New York. She finally had her own home. But Harriet did not rest. She spent many years fighting for the rights of women. Later, she helped build a home on her land where old, poor black people could live.

On March 10, 1913, Harriet died. She was over ninety years old. She had been born a slave but never gave up on her dream of freedom. Harriet was a hero to everyone she saved from slavery, and her bravery and strength continue to inspire people today.

Harriet Says:

"I never ran my train off track and I never lost a passenger."

Timeline

About 1820—Harriet is born on a plantation in Maryland.

1844—Harriet marries John Tubman.

1849—Harriet runs away from the plantation to Pennsylvania.

1850—Harriet becomes a conductor on the Underground Railroad, helping slaves to escape.

1857—Harriet rescues her parents and takes them to Canada.

1861–1865—Harriet works as a nurse, spy, and scout during the Civil War.

1863—President Lincoln frees the slaves on January 1.

1869—Harriet marries Nelson Davis.

1908—Harriet builds a home for poor and old black people in Auburn, New York.

1913—Harriet Tubman dies on March 10.

Learn More

Books

McDonough, Yona Zeldis. ***What Was the Underground Railroad?*** New York: Grosset & Dunlap, 2013.

Norwich, Grace. ***I Am Harriet Tubman.*** New York: Scholastic, 2013.

Pace, Lorenzo. ***Harriet Tubman and My Grandmother's Quilts.*** New York: Windmill Books, 2015.

Web Sites

education.nationalgeographic.com/education/maps/undergroundrailroad/?ar_a=1

Includes background information and a detailed map of the Underground Railroad.

harriet-tubman.org

Learn about the life and times of Harriet Tubman through stories, pictures, maps, and videos.

Index

Published in 2016 by Enslow Publishing, LLC.
101 W. 23rd Street, Suite 240, New York, NY 10011

Library of Congress Cataloging-in-Publication Data

Taylor, Charlotte, 1978-
Harriet Tubman : hero of the Underground Railroad / Charlotte Taylor and Stephen Feinstein.
pages cm. — (Exceptional African Americans)
Includes bibliographical references and index.
Summary: "A biography of abolitionist Harriet Tubman"—Provided by publisher.
Audience: Grades 4-6.
ISBN 978-0-7660-7128-5 (library binding)
ISBN 978-0-7660-7126-1 (pbk.)
ISBN 978-0-7660-7127-8 (6-pack)
1. Tubman, Harriet, 1820?-1913—Juvenile literature. 2. Slaves—United States—Biography—Juvenile literature. 3. African American women—Biography—Juvenile literature. 4. African Americans—Biography—Juvenile literature. 5. Underground Railroad—Juvenile literature. I. Feinstein, Stephen. II. Title.
E444.T82T393 2015
326.8092—dc23
[B]
2015007449

Printed in the United States of America

To Our Readers: We have done our best to make sure all Web sitwe addresses in this book were active and appropriate when we went to press. However, the author and the publisher have no control over and assume no liability for the material available on those Web sites or on any Web sites they may link to. Any comments or suggestions can be sent by e-mail to customerservice@enslow.com.

Photo Credits: Getty Images: Print Collector/Hulton Archive, p. 4; SuperStock, pp. 10, 14; MPI/Archive Photos, p. 18; Afro Newspaper/Gato/Archive Photos, p. 19; From p. 79 of Kate Clifford Larson's *Bound for the Promised Land/Cambridge Democrat*, 1849, p. 16; Library of Congress Prints and Photographs Division, Washington, D.C.: pp. 1, 7, 9, 11, 20; ©Toria/Shutterstock.com (blue background throughout book).

Cover Credits: Library of Congress Prints and Photographs Division, Washington, D.C. (portrait of Harriet Tubman); ©Toria/Shutterstock.com (blue background).